BUG OFF!

A Swarm
of Insect Words

Cathi Hepworth

SCHOLASTIC INC.
New York   Toronto   London   Auckland   Sydney
Mexico City   New Delhi   Hong Kong

For Bill and Mike,
who are as cute as a bug's ear!

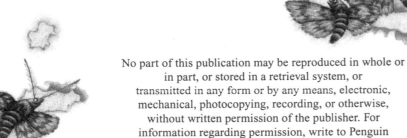

ISBN 0-439-06194-6

Copyright © 1998 by Catherine Hepworth.
All rights reserved. Published by Scholastic Inc.,
555 Broadway, New York, NY 10012, by arrangement
with Penguin Putnam Inc.
SCHOLASTIC and associated logos are trademarks and/or
registered trademarks of Scholastic Inc.

12 11 10 9 8 7 6 5 4 3 2   9/9 0 1 2 3 4/0

Printed in the U.S.A.   24

First Scholastic printing, October 1999

Text set in Times Roman.

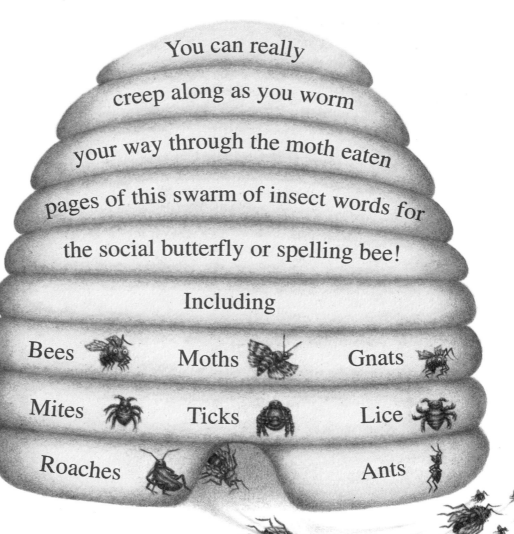

You can really

creep along as you worm

your way through the moth eaten

pages of this swarm of insect words for

the social butterfly or spelling bee!

Including

Bees   Moths   Gnats

Mites   Ticks   Lice

Roaches   Ants

*A Real
Fly-by-Night
Operation...*

Starring

Bees, Moths, and Gnats

B e eper

Fris**bee**

Bee**t**hoven

Bee**f**y

Mam**moth**

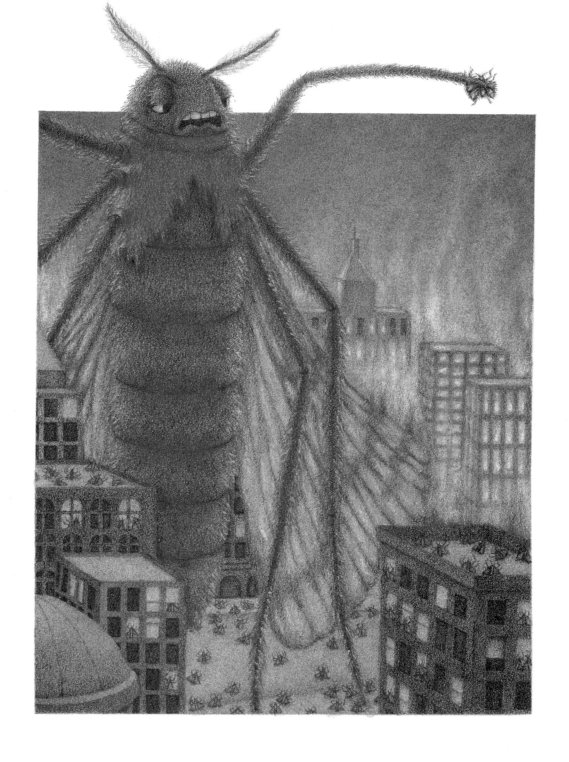

Behe**moth**

Smoth**ered**

Signatures

Stagnate

Don't Let the Bedbugs Bite...

Starring

Mites, Ticks, and Lice

Stalag**mite**s

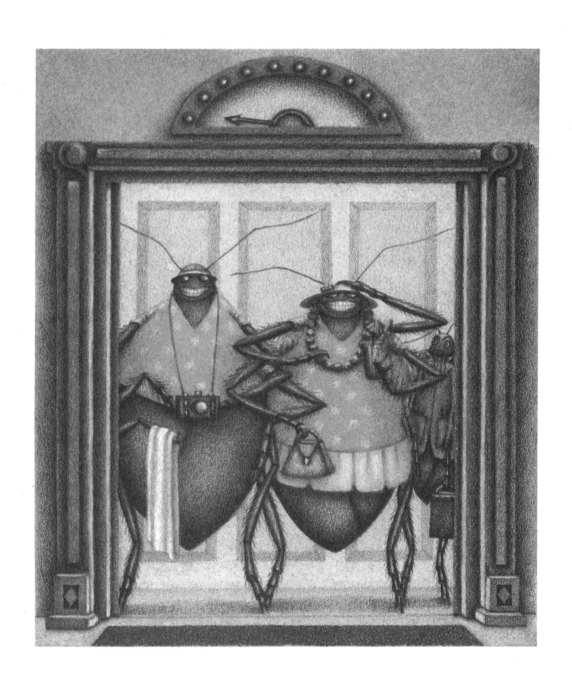

Encroach

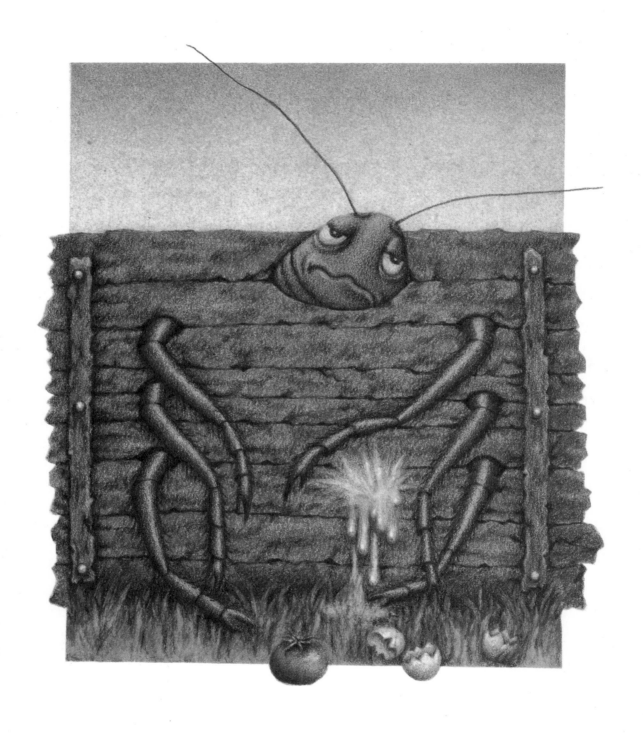

Rep**ro**ach

App**roach**

The Unwelcome Houseguests...

Starring

Roaches and Ants

Slice

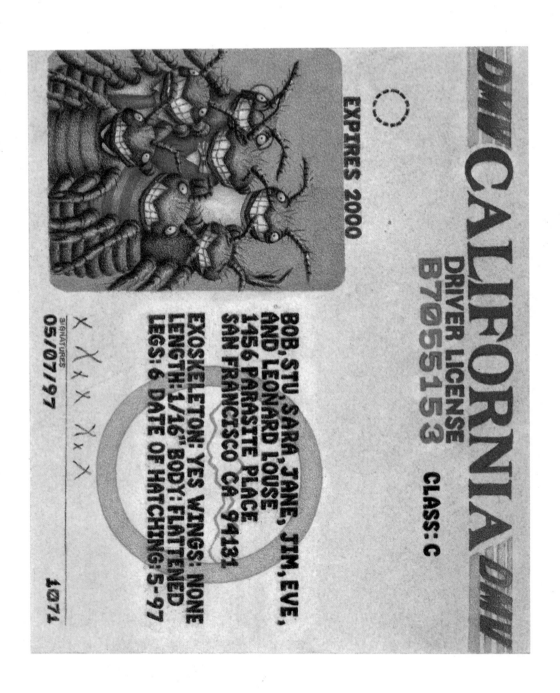

License

Tick-tack-toe

Broom**stick**

Ticklish

Dyna**mite**

Frantic

Romantic

Descend**ant**s

Slant**e**d

Phantom of the Opera